Quick & Easy

Quick & Easy

Bounty
Books

First published in Great Britain in 1999 by
Hamlyn, a division of Octopus Publishing
Group Ltd

This edition published in 2007 by Bounty Books, a
division of Octopus Publishing Group Ltd
2–4 Heron Quays, London E14 4JP
Reprinted 2008 (twice)
An Hachette Livre UK Company

Copyright © Octopus Publishing Group Ltd 1999

All rights reserved. No part of this work may be
reproduced or utilized in any form or by any
means, electronic or mechanical, including
photocopying, recording or by any information
storage and retrieval system, without the
prior written permission of the publisher

ISBN: 978-0-753716-27-4

A CIP catalogue record for this book is available
from the British Library

Printed and bound in China

Notes

1 Standard level spoon measurements are used in all recipes.

1 tablespoon = one 15 ml spoon
1 teaspoon = one 5 ml spoon

2 Both imperial and metric measurements have been given in all recipes. Use one set of measurements only and not a mixture of both.

3 Measurements for canned food have been given as a standard metric equivalent.

4 Eggs should be medium unless otherwise stated. The Department of Health advises that eggs should not be consumed raw. This book may contain dishes made with lightly cooked eggs. It is prudent for more vulnerable people, such as pregnant and nursing mothers, invalids, the elderly, babies and young children, to avoid uncooked or lightly cooked dishes made with eggs. Once prepared, these dishes should be used immediately.

5 Milk should be full fat unless otherwise stated.

6 Poultry should be cooked thoroughly. To test if poultry is cooked, piece the flesh through the thickest part with a skewer or fork – the juices should run clear, never pink or red.

7 Fresh herbs should be used unless otherwise stated. If unavailable, use dried herbs as an alternative but halve the quantities stated.

8 Pepper should be freshly ground black pepper unless otherwise stated; season according to taste.

9 Ovens should be preheated to the specified temperature – if using a fan-assisted oven, follow the manufacturer's instructions for adjusting the time and the temperature.

10 Do not refreeze a dish that has been frozen previously.

11 This book includes dishes made with nuts and nut derivatives. It is advisable for customers with known allergic reactions to nuts and nut derivatives and those who may be potentially vulnerable to these allergies, such as pregnant and nursing mothers, invalids, the elderly, babies and children, to avoid dishes made with nuts and nut oils. It is also prudent to check the labels of pre-prepared ingredients for the possible inclusion of nut derivatives.

12 Vegetarians should look for the 'V' symbol on a cheese to ensure it is made with vegetarian rennet. There are vegetarian forms of Parmesan, feta, Cheddar, Cheshire, red Leicester, dolcelatte and many goats' cheeses, among others.

For something quick, easy and delicious when you don't want to spend hours in the kitchen, rethink soups, starters and snacks with the recipes in this chapter.

Put a bit of spice in your life and adventure in your cooking with these recipes. Experience flavours from the four corners of the globe without stepping out of your kitchen.

For formal and informal occasions this chapter will provide you with the answer, with a whole host of flavours for exciting fish and tasty meat dishes.

Salads are no longer simply seen as just an accompaniment to a meal, they can be a meal in their own right. Excite the senses by combining different flavours and textures, colours and tastes.

Tantalize your tastebuds with these sweet things, the perfect end to a meal or simply a little bit of indulgence to keep you going through the day.

contents

6

introduction

What with the speed of modern life and the aspirations that glossy magazines and television programmes hold up to us, it seems that many of us are trying to cram several lifestyles into every day – worker, homemaker, parent and even semi-athlete, attending regular workouts in the gym. As we dash here and there, always trying to keep up with the clock, it's tempting to pluck a ready-made meal off the shelf as we hurry round the supermarket and drop it in the shopping trolley – no mess, no cooking and hardly any washing up. Even the keenest cook has evenings when there simply isn't an hour to spare for making a meal.

Yet quick meals don't have to mean opening a package and reheating the contents – it's quite possible to put together a homemade meal in a matter of minutes and it'll taste that much better, full of nutrients and fresh flavours. Now that our supermarkets stock ingredients used in other cuisines worldwide, the choice of dish that can be placed on the table with minimum fuss is wider than ever. In this book you'll find recipes such as Risotto alla Parmigiana from Italy (see page 34), Prawn and Mango Curry from India (see page 42), Chickpea and Chard Tortilla from Mexico (see page 37), Rapid-fried Prawns from China (see page 40) and Thai Red Beef Curry (see page 44). None of them is complicated and none will send you searching for hard-to-find ingredients, but they will add zingy flavours and a touch of pizzazz to mealtimes.

Storecupboard staples

The essence of quick and easy cooking is having a good stock of ingredients that you can draw on when time is too short to do much shopping. Keeping a selection of pastas means that all you need do is whip up a sauce to make a hot and filling meal and, while fresh pasta is best, the dried varieties are more than acceptable when fresh isn't readily available. Canned tomatoes are invaluable for making a pasta sauce, to which you can add any vegetables you have to hand. Pine nuts are pricey, but a few go a very long way and they are wonderful with pasta – you'll find them in Pappardelle with Pesto and Potatoes (see page 30) and Spaghetti with Leeks and Pine Nuts (see page 32).

Ready-made pizza bases offer another option for an Italian meal in a moment. Mozzarella cheese is the classic starting point for a pizza filling, but these days pizzas have come a long way from their origins and may be found with almost anything on top. Put by a jar of capers and a tin or two of anchovies – they take up hardly any room in the cupboard, but the flavour they impart is way out of proportion to their size.

Rice is now available in a range of types: easy-cook, basmati, Thai jasmine rice, arborio rice for risottos, red Camargue rice, brown rice and wild rice – though the latter is in fact not a real rice at all but a type of wild grass native to North America. Basic patna rice comes either long-grain or short-grain, the latter used mainly for dessert dishes. The recipes featured in this book use three different types of rice –

'Many's the long night I've dreamed of
Cheese - toasted mostly.'

Robert Louis Stevenson

long-grain, basmati and arborio – but don't stop there. Explore them all, and the different cooking methods that different nations use to cook them, from the sticky rice of China to the 'dried down' rice of the Caribbean.

Pulses of all types are highly nutritious, cheap and filling. Cooking the dried type needs some forethought as most require a period of soaking and then a further hour or so of simmering, but canned chickpeas, black-eyed peas, lentils, flageolet beans, cannellini beans, kidney beans and aduki beans are readily available. Pulses are endlessly versatile and can crop up in curries or in salads such as Char-grilled Pasta Salad (see page 20), so they are equally useful for an *al fresco* summer lunch or a warming winter supper.

Spicing it up

Other essentials for making a quick meal an interesting one too are spices and flavourings such as fish sauce (nam pla) and soy sauce. A basic spice collection might consist of cumin, coriander, turmeric, chilli powder, garam masala and cloves – if you become enthused about cooking curries you can go on to add the more unusual spices to make a full set. Coconut milk, which is used widely in Indian, Oriental and Caribbean dishes, can be bought in packets or in cans. In this book you'll find it adding its characteristic flavour and texture to Coconut Rice with Fish and Peas (see page 38), Simple Beef Curry with Spinach (see page 45), Prawn and Mango Curry (see page 42) and Thai Red Beef Curry (see page 44).

Herbs are best bought fresh and are increasingly sold still growing in their pots. Nevertheless, it does no harm to have a few jars of dried herbs for those days when no fresh ones are to be found, though dried parsley is never a good option.

A fresh approach

Once you have got your storecupboard established, all you need for a range of quick meals is some fresh produce. Use vegetables and salad ingredients as soon as possible after buying them, as they begin to lose their nutrients as soon as they are lifted from the earth. Cook vegetables for the minimum amount of time, just until they are tender – their flavour and texture is infinitely superior to that of overcooked vegetables. Take them from the heat before they lose their fresh colour and serve immediately, full of goodness. Cooking quick and easy meals with maximum success is a matter of getting the timing right, using good ingredients, mastering such recipes as the ones in this book, and then going on to experiment with some of your own. You'll soon be passing the convenience foods on the supermarket shelves without a second glance!

cream of celery & prawn soup •

omelettes à la crème •

goats' cheese & cherry tomato puff tart •

herby sausage patties •

burger pitta pockets •

grilled mushrooms with garlic oil •

char-grilled pasta salad •

jacket potato with broccoli, corn & cheese •

smoky chillied prawns •

tuna fish cakes •

baked brie with cranberries •

blt sandwich •

cheesy leek & herb scones •

soups, starters & snacks

cream of celery & prawn soup

1 Mix the can of celery soup and the milk in a saucepan. Add the paprika and white pepper. Bring to simmering point and simmer, stirring constantly, for 5 minutes. Take the pan off the heat.

2 If serving the soup hot, stir in the yogurt and prawns and reheat gently for about 2 minutes. Do not boil. Serve the soup in heated bowls, garnishing each portion with snipped chives and a sprinkling of paprika.

3 If serving the soup chilled, pour the soup into a bowl and leave to cool. Stir in the yogurt and prawns, cover the bowl and chill in the refrigerator for at least 3 hours. Serve the soup in chilled bowls, garnishing each portion with snipped chives and a sprinkling of paprika.

300 g (10 oz) can condensed cream of celery soup

300 ml (½ pint) milk

1 teaspoon paprika, extra for sprinkling

½ teaspoon white pepper

2 tablespoons natural yogurt

150 g (5 oz) cooked peeled prawns, thoroughly defrosted if frozen

snipped fresh chives, to garnish

Serves 2–3
Preparation time: 3–5 minutes, plus chilling
Cooking time: 5–7 minutes

■ This fragrant, smooth soup may be served hot or chilled and takes only minutes to prepare.

omelettes à la crème

1 Heat the grill to high. Mix together 125 g (4 oz) cheese and 3 tablespoons cream. In a separate bowl, beat 6 eggs with 140 ml (4½ fl oz) water and season to taste with salt and pepper.

2 Melt 50 g (2 oz) butter in a large omelette pan and when sizzling pour in the egg mixture. When the omelette begins to set, draw the edges gently into the centre of the pan and allow the liquid egg to run underneath, using a wooden spatula. When the omelette is almost set, but still creamy, spread it out to the sides of the pan and allow it to set completely.

3 Spoon half the cheese and cream mixture down the centre of the omelette. Arrange 4 asparagus spears on one half of the omelette and fold the other half over, to cover. Slide the omelette carefully on to a flameproof plate.

4 Cover the omelette with the remaining cheese mixture. Place under the grill for several seconds until the cheese is bubbling. Keep warm while preparing the second omelette in the same way. Garnish the omelettes with watercress and tomato, if liked. Each omelette serves 2, so cut them in half before serving on warmed individual plates.

250 g (8 oz) Cheddar cheese, grated

6 tablespoons single cream

12 eggs

275 ml (9 fl oz) water

125 g (4 oz) butter

8 asparagus spears, lightly steamed

salt and pepper

Serves 4
Preparation time: 6 minutes
Cooking time: 8 minutes

goats' cheese & cherry tomato puff tart

1 Roll out the pastry on a lightly floured surface and trim to a 23 cm (9 inch) round. Place on a greased baking sheet and brush lightly with olive oil.

2 Spread half the cherry tomatoes over the pastry to within 2.5 cm (1 inch) of the edge. Arrange the goats' cheese over the top and sprinkle with the remaining tomatoes. Season with a little salt and pepper. Sprinkle with the chopped thyme and drizzle olive oil over the top.

3 Bake in a preheated oven, 220°C (425°F), Gas Mark 7, for 20–25 minutes, until the pastry is risen, crisp and golden brown.

250 g (8 oz) puff pastry, thawed if frozen

1–2 tablespoons olive oil

250 g (8 oz) cherry tomatoes, prefer- ably a mixture of red and yellow, sliced

250 g (8 oz) firm goats' cheese, sliced

2 teaspoons chopped thyme

salt and pepper

Serves 4–6

Preparation time: 15 minutes

Cooking time: 20–25 minutes

■ Serve this delicious tart hot, either as a starter or for a light lunch accompanied by a salad of bitter leaves.

herby sausage patties

1 Mix together the sausagemeat, mixed herbs, Worcestershire sauce and salt and pepper to taste. Form the mixture into 4 patties.

2 Heat a little oil in a frying pan. Add the patties and cook for 3–4 minutes on one side, then turn them and cook for 4–5 minutes more until browned and cooked through.

3 Meanwhile, split the baps in half and toast the cut sides. Spread them with butter and a little mustard and serve each sausage patty between two bap halves, topped with onion rings, if liked, and a side salad.

500 g (1 lb) pork sausagemeat

1 teaspoon mixed dried herbs

1 tablespoon Worcestershire sauce

oil, for frying

4 baps

softened butter, for spreading

prepared English mustard

salt and pepper

side salad, to garnish (optional)

Serves 4

Preparation time: 10 minutes

Cooking time: 10 minutes

burger pitta pockets

1 Mix the margarine and relish together in a small bowl and set aside. Heat the oil in a large frying pan, add the hamburgers and cook for 3 minutes, turning once. Add the onion rings and fry for 2 minutes. Transfer the hamburgers and onion to a plate, using a spatula.

2 Make a slit lengthways down one side of each pitta bread and open to form a pocket. Spread the margarine and relish mixture inside and over the top. Put all the pittas on a large piece of foil. Add the mini hamburgers, the cherry tomatoes and a few onion rings to each one. Wrap the foil around the pittas to cover them completely and place the foil parcel on a baking sheet. Place in a preheated oven, 190°C (375°F), Gas Mark 5, and heat for 10 minutes.

3 Remove the baking sheet from the oven and fold back the foil so that the tops of the pittas are uncovered. Return them to the oven for a further 5 minutes to crisp up.

4 When the tops are crisp, remove from the oven and add the diced cucumber. Arrange the pittas on a serving plate. Corn salad makes a good accompaniment. Serve hot.

3 tablespoons soft margarine

1 tablespoon tomato, corn or chilli relish

2 teaspoons corn oil

16 mini hamburger patties

1 large onion, sliced and separated into rings

4 large pitta breads

8 cherry tomatoes

5 cm (2 inch) piece of cucumber, diced

Makes 4

Preparation time: 15 minutes

Cooking time: 20 minutes

18

grilled mushrooms
with garlic oil

1 In a small bowl, combine all the ingredients except the flat mushrooms and season to taste with salt and pepper.

2 Arrange the mushrooms stalk side down on a foil-lined grill pan and cook under a preheated grill, as close to the heat as possible, for 3–4 minutes until they are beginning to moisten.

3 Flip the mushrooms over and cook for a further 4–5 minutes until cooked through. Transfer to a serving plate and pour the dressing over them. Set the mushrooms aside to cool to room temperature. Serve with lime wedges.

75 ml (3 fl oz) extra virgin olive oil

2 garlic cloves, crushed

grated rind and juice of ½ lime

1 small red chilli, deseeded and finely chopped

2 tablespoons chopped parsley

12 large flat mushrooms

salt and pepper

lime wedges, to serve

Serves 4

Preparation time: 5 minutes plus cooling

Cooking time: 8–10 minutes

char-grilled pasta salad

1 Spread out the aubergine slices on some baking sheets and sprinkle with the salt. Set aside for 15 minutes.

2 Meanwhile, bring the measured water to the boil in a large saucepan. Add a dash of oil and a generous pinch of salt. Cook the pasta for 8–12 minutes, until just tender. Drain and rinse under cold water in a colander. Drain again, transfer to a large salad bowl and set aside.

3 Rinse the aubergine slices under plenty of cold water, drain and pat dry with kitchen paper. Grill under a high heat for 10 minutes until crisp, turning once. Alternatively, grill over hot coals, turning once, for 5 minutes until coloured. Slice each aubergine round in half. Set aside.

4 In a bowl, whisk the remaining olive oil with the vinegar and Dijon mustard. Add salt and pepper to taste. Add the dressing to the pasta and toss well. Fold in the celery, kidney beans and aubergine slices. Scatter the celery leaves on top to garnish and serve at once.

1 large aubergine, sliced

1 tablespoon salt

2 litres (3¼ pints) water

150 ml (¼ pint) olive oil

250 g (8 oz) dried penne rigate

6 tablespoons balsamic vinegar

1 teaspoon Dijon mustard

2 celery sticks, chopped

150 g (5 oz) canned red kidney beans, drained

salt and pepper

1 tablespoon chopped celery leaves, to garnish

Serves 4

Preparation time: 20 minutes, plus standing

Cooking time: 12 minutes

jacket potato with broccoli, corn & cheese

1 Cut the broccoli into small florets and cook in lightly salted boiling water until just tender. Drain well in a colander.

2 Cut the potatoes in half and scoop out the flesh, leaving a thick shell. Chop the flesh and add the butter, broccoli and sweetcorn. Season generously with salt and pepper and spoon back into the potatoes.

3 Sprinkle with the cheese and place under a preheated grill until just melted. Serve hot.

150 g (5 oz) broccoli

4 baked potatoes

15 g (½ oz) butter

200 g (7 oz) can sweetcorn, drained

4 tablespoons grated Edam cheese

salt and pepper

Serves 4

Preparation time: 10 minutes

Cooking time: 12 minutes

1. Wrap one half of each chilli round the middle of each prawn then thread 5 prawns on each of 4 metal or soaked bamboo skewers.

2. Place the skewers in a long shallow dish and sprinkle with the oil and sea salt. Cover the dish and leave to marinate in a cool place for about 30 minutes.

3. Cook the prawns on the oiled grill of a preheated barbecue or under a preheated grill for 3 minutes on each side, basting with any remaining marinade. Serve the prawns hot with lemon wedges.

10 green chillies, halved lengthways and deseeded

20 raw king prawns, peeled with the tails left on

5 tablespoons olive oil

coarsely ground sea salt

lemon wedges, to serve

Serves 4
Preparation time: 15 minutes, plus marinating
Cooking time: 6 minutes

smoky chillied prawns

tuna fish cakes

1 Mash the potatoes in a bowl with the butter or margarine, then mix in the tuna, parsley, salt and pepper to taste and half of the beaten egg. Cover the mixture and chill in the refrigerator for 20 minutes.

2 Place the tuna mixture on a floured surface and shape into a roll. Cut into 8 slices and shape each one into a flat round about 6 cm (2½ inches) in diameter. Dip the rounds into the remaining egg, then coat with breadcrumbs.

3 Heat the oil in a frying pan, add the fish cakes and fry for 2–3 minutes on each side or until golden brown and heated through. Serve with a tomato and onion salad.

300 g (10 oz) potatoes, boiled

25 g (1 oz) butter or margarine

300 g (10 oz) canned tuna, drained and flaked

2 tablespoons chopped parsley

2 eggs, beaten

75 g (3 oz) dry breadcrumbs

oil, for shallow-frying

salt and pepper

tomato and onion salad, to serve

Serves 4

Preparation time: 10–15 minutes, plus chilling

Cooking time: 12 minutes

baked brie with cranberries

1 To make the relish, place the cranberries together with the grated orange rind and juice, ginger and sugar in a blender or food processor and process to a coarse purée. Leave to stand for 1 hour before serving.

2 To make the baked Brie, mix the toasted breadcrumbs with the parsley, thyme and dried cranberries. Dip each piece of Brie into the beaten egg and then coat evenly with the breadcrumb mixture.

3 Lay the pieces of coated Brie on a greased baking sheet and place on the middle shelf of a pre-heated oven, 220°C (425°F), Gas Mark 7, for 8 minutes. Remove the Brie from the oven and leave to cool briefly.

4 Arrange the rocket or lettuce leaves on 4 plates. Spoon some cranberry relish on to the plates and place the warm Brie on slices of toasted French bread that have been rubbed with cut garlic and extra cranberry relish. Garnish with chives.

Baked Brie:

25 g (1 oz) toasted fresh breadcrumbs

1 tablespoon chopped parsley

1 teaspoon chopped thyme

1 tablespoon dried cranberries, finely chopped

4 x 50 g (2 oz) pieces of Brie

1 egg, beaten

Relish:

250 g (8 oz) cranberries, defrosted if frozen

3 tablespoons grated orange rind

65 ml (2½ fl oz) orange juice

1 cm (½ inch) piece of fresh root ginger, peeled and grated

100 g (3½ oz) sugar

To Serve:

rocket or assorted lettuce leaves

4 thick slices of French bread, toasted

1 garlic clove, cut in half lengthways

snipped fresh chives

Serves 4

Preparation time: 25 minutes, plus standing

Cooking time: 10 minutes

blt sandwich

1 Cook the bacon in a small frying pan until golden brown and crisp, turning once. Remove and drain on kitchen paper.

2 Spread the toast with mayonnaise and arrange the bacon, tomato and lettuce over one slice. Season with salt and pepper and top with the remaining toast slice. Serve hot or cold.

■ For a tasty variation use rye or white bread and place a slice of Cheddar cheese on top of the toast. Grill until bubbling then place the remaining ingredients on top, omitting the mayonnaise.

2 lean bacon rashers

2 slices of wholemeal or multi-grain bread, toasted

2 tablespoons mayonnaise

3 cherry tomatoes, halved

about 4 baby lettuce leaves

salt and pepper

Makes 1
Preparation time: 5 minutes
Cooking time: 5–7 minutes

cheesy leek & herb scones

1 Sift the flour, bicarbonate of soda, cream of tartar and salt into a bowl. Cut the butter into small pieces and rub it into the flour until the mixture resembles fine bread-crumbs. Stir in half the Cheddar, the leek or chives, parsley, basil or marjoram and pepper.

2 Make a well in the centre and add almost all the buttermilk, mixing with a wooden spoon or broad-bladed knife to form a soft dough. Take care not to overwork the dough or it will be heavy and tough. Turn on to a lightly floured surface and knead very gently to form a round shape. Pat or roll to about 2–2.5 cm (¾–1 inch) thick, then cut into scones using a 4.5 cm (1¾ inch) pastry cutter.

3 Place the scones a few centimetres apart on a lightly floured baking sheet and brush with a little egg or milk to glaze. Top with the remaining cheese and a light dusting of paprika. Place in a pre-heated oven, 220°C (425°F), Gas Mark 7 for 15–20 minutes until well risen and light golden in colour. Serve hot or cold, with butter.

250 g (8 oz) plain flour, plus extra for dusting

1 teaspoon bicarbonate of soda

1 teaspoon cream of tartar

25 g (1 oz) butter, plus extra to serve

50–75 g (2–3 oz) mature farmhouse Cheddar cheese, grated

2 tablespoons finely chopped leek or snipped chives

1 tablespoon finely chopped parsley

1 teaspoon finely chopped basil or marjoram

200 ml (7 fl oz) buttermilk

beaten egg or milk, to glaze

salt and pepper

paprika, for dusting

Makes 15

Preparation time: 15 minutes

Cooking time: 15–20 minutes

around the world

pappardelle with pesto & potatoes

1 Cook the potatoes in a pan of lightly salted boiling water for 15–20 minutes until just tender. Drain the potatoes, dry them on kitchen paper, then place them in a shallow dish with the olive oil and salt and toss gently to coat with the oil.

2 Bring the measured water to the boil in a large saucepan. Add a dash of oil and a generous pinch of salt. Add the pasta and cook for 4–8 minutes or according to packet instructions until just tender.

3 Drain the pasta well and transfer to a warm serving bowl. Add the potatoes and pesto and toss thoroughly. Garnish with the pine nuts and parsley and serve with a mixed green salad.

375 g (12 oz) new potatoes or large red-skinned potatoes, cut into chunks

2 tablespoons olive oil

1 tablespoon coarse salt

1.8 litres (3 pints) water

300 g (10 oz) fresh pappardelle

250 g (8 oz) ready-made pesto

salt and pepper

To Garnish:

2 tablespoons toasted pine nuts

2 tablespoons finely chopped parsley

Serves 4
Preparation time: 15 minutes
Cooking time: 20–30 minutes

spaghetti with leeks & pine nuts

1 Trim the roots, coarse outer leaves and green tops from the leeks; cut the white parts into rings, wash under running water and drain well.

2 Heat the butter and oil in a large pan over a low heat. Add the leeks, onion, bacon and pine nuts and cook until golden. Add the spinach, season with salt and pepper and sprinkle with the wine. Allow the wine to evaporate, then add the passata. Simmer until the sauce has reduced a little then add the cream. Stir and leave on a very low heat for about 10 minutes.

3 Meanwhile, cook the pasta in boiling salted water until tender. Drain, pour the sauce on top and mix well. Serve the pasta sprinkled with Parmesan cheese.

3 leeks

50 g (2 oz) butter

2 tablespoons oil

½ onion, chopped

50 g (2 oz) bacon, diced

2 tablespoons chopped pine nuts

125 g (4 oz) frozen spinach, thawed

3 tablespoons dry white wine

200 g (7 oz) canned passata (sieved tomatoes)

3 tablespoons single cream

375 g (12 oz) spaghetti

25 g (1 oz) Parmesan cheese, grated

salt and pepper

Serves 4
Preparation time: 10 minutes
Cooking time: 25 minutes

chicago pizza

1 Melt the butter in a pan, add the onions and cook for 5 minutes. Leave to cool. When they are cool spread the tomato purée on the pizza base, then make a layer of onions and pepperoni. Sprinkle with the thyme, marjoram, Bel Paese and mozzarella.

2 Bake at once in a preheated oven, 220°C (425°F), Gas Mark 7, for 15–20 minutes, until the dough and topping are golden. Garnish with marjoram and serve immediately.

25 g (1 oz) butter

2 onions, sliced

4 tablespoons tomato purée

1 ready-made 30 cm (12 inch) pizza base

50 g (2 oz) pepperoni, sliced

1 tablespoon chopped thyme

1 tablespoon chopped marjoram

25 g (1 oz) Bel Paese cheese, diced

25 g (1 oz) mozzarella cheese, diced

marjoram sprigs, to garnish

Serves 4
Preparation time: 10 minutes, plus cooling
Cooking time: 20–25 minutes

risotto alla Parmigiana

1 Melt 50 g (2 oz) of the butter in a heavy-based pan, add the onion and fry gently for 5 minutes until softened. Season to taste with pepper, then add the wine and boil briskly until it has evaporated.

2 Add the rice and cook, stirring, for 1–2 minutes until it has absorbed the onion and wine mixture. Add a ladleful of the hot stock and cook over medium-low heat, stirring, until it has been absorbed. Continue adding the stock, a ladleful at a time, stirring constantly and adding more only when the previous addition has just been absorbed. When all the stock has been absorbed (this will take about 20–25 minutes), remove the pan from the heat, add the remaining butter and the grated Parmesan, and fold them in gently.

3 Transfer to warmed plates, sprinkle with the Parmesan shavings and a generous grinding of black pepper, and serve immediately with radicchio and rocket leaves.

125 g (4 oz) unsalted butter, softened

1 onion, finely chopped

3–4 tablespoons dry white wine

400 g (13 oz) arborio risotto rice

1 litre (1¾ pints) hot beef stock, kept simmering

125 g (4 oz) Parmesan cheese, grated

Parmesan shavings, to garnish

Serves 4–6
Preparation time: 5–10 minutes
Cooking time: 25–30 minutes

■ Use only the best quality Parmesan cheese for this recipe and grate it just before you add it to the dish.

chicken &
carrot rice

1 Wash the basmati rice thoroughly under cold running water, then soak in plenty of cold water for about 30 minutes. Drain well.

2 Mix the chilli powder and ½ teaspoon of salt on a plate and lightly dip the chicken pieces in the mixture. Heat 25 g (1 oz) of the butter in a frying pan, add the coated chicken strips and garlic and stir-fry for about 2 minutes.

3 Heat the remaining butter in a large pan, add the onion, almonds and raisins and fry until golden and lightly browned. Stir in the turmeric, then the drained rice and fry, stirring, for 1–2 minutes. Season well with salt, then stir in the carrots, the chicken strips and the stock. Bring to the boil, cover the frying pan with a tight-fitting lid, reduce the heat to very low and simmer for about 20 minutes or until the rice is cooked and all the liquid has been absorbed. Transfer the chicken and carrot rice to a large, warmed serving dish and serve, garnished with coriander sprigs.

375 g (12 oz) basmati rice

1 teaspoon chilli powder

3 skinless, boneless chicken breasts, cut into strips

75 g (3 oz) butter

2 garlic cloves, finely chopped

1 onion, sliced

50 g (2 oz) almonds, halved

50 g (2 oz) raisins

1 teaspoon turmeric

500 g (1 lb) carrots, grated

450 ml (¾ pint) chicken stock

salt

fresh coriander sprigs, to garnish

Serves 4

Preparation time: 15 minutes plus standing

Cooking time: 30 minutes

chickpea &
chard tortilla

1. Heat 4 tablespoons of the oil in a large nonstick, heavy-based frying pan. Add the onion, garlic and chilli flakes and fry gently for 10 minutes until softened and lightly golden.

2. Meanwhile, wash and dry the chard and cut away and discard the thick white central stalk. Shred the leaves. Stir the chard into the onion mixture together with the chickpeas and cook gently for 5 minutes.

3. Beat the eggs in a bowl, add the parsley and season with salt and pepper. Stir in the chickpea mixture. Wipe out the pan, then add the remaining oil. Pour in the egg and chickpea tortilla mixture and cook over a low heat for 10 minutes until the tortilla is almost cooked through.

4. Carefully slide the tortilla out on to a large plate, invert the pan over the tortilla and then flip it back into the pan. Return the pan to the heat and continue to cook for a further 5 minutes until cooked through. Allow to cool to room temperature and serve cut into squares.

6 tablespoons extra virgin olive oil

1 onion, chopped

4 garlic cloves, crushed

½ teaspoon crushed chilli flakes

500 g (1 lb) chard leaves

425 g (14 oz) can chickpeas, drained

6 eggs, beaten

2 tablespoons chopped parsley

salt and pepper

Serves 12

Preparation time: 10 minutes, plus cooling

Cooking time: 30 minutes

coconut rice with fish & peas

1 Melt 15 g (½ oz) of the butter in a large frying pan, add the spices, stir well and then add the fish. Fry for 1–2 minutes until golden on all sides and carefully remove from the pan with a slotted spoon. Set aside.

2 Add the remaining butter to the pan and fry the onion and garlic for 5 minutes. Add the rice, stir well until all the grains are glossy, and then add the tomatoes, stock and coconut milk. Bring to the boil, cover and simmer for 15 minutes. Stir in the peas, adjust the seasoning if necessary and arrange the fish over the top. Cover with foil and then the lid and continue to cook for 5 minutes. Leave to stand for a further 5 minutes.

3 Transfer to warm serving bowls, garnish with chopped coriander or parsley and some coriander sprigs. Serve at once.

■ Use monkfish, if possible, as the flesh is firm and less likely to disintegrate than that of cod. If you do use cod, sprinkle with salt and leave for 1 hour to firm up the flesh, then wash well and pat dry.

25 g (1 oz) butter

1 teaspoon ground coriander

½ teaspoon turmeric

¼ teaspoon ground cinnamon

½ teaspoon pepper

375g (12 oz) monkfish or skinless cod fillet, washed, dried and cut into bite-sized pieces

1 onion, chopped

1 garlic clove, crushed

250 g (8 oz) long-grain rice, washed

400 g (13 oz) can chopped tomatoes

300 ml (½ pint) vegetable stock

200ml (7 fl oz) coconut milk

125 g (4 oz) peas, thawed if frozen

To Garnish:

1 tablespoon chopped coriander or parsley

coriander sprigs

Serves 4
Preparation time: 10 minutes
Cooking time: 30 minutes

stir-fried monkfish with noodles

1 Blend the egg white, sherry and cornflour together in a dish. Add the fish and toss well. Set aside for several hours or overnight.

2 Strain the fish from its marinade. Combine the sauce ingredients together and set aside. Cook the noodles according to the packet instructions, drain well and set aside.

3 Heat the two oils in a wok or large frying pan and stir-fry the fish over a high heat for 2 minutes until golden. Remove from the pan with a slotted spoon.

4 Add the garlic, ginger, orange rind, leek and red pepper to the pan and stir-fry for 3 minutes. Add the water chestnuts, bean sprouts, cooked noodles, sauce and fish to the pan and simmer gently for 2 minutes until all the vegetables and the fish are heated through. Serve at once.

1 egg white, beaten lightly

1 tablespoon dry sherry

1 tablespoon cornflour

750 g (1½ lb) monkfish fillet, washed, dried and cubed

125 g (4 oz) dried egg thread noodles

2 tablespoons sunflower oil

2 teaspoons sesame oil

1 garlic clove, sliced

2.5 cm (1 inch) piece of fresh root ginger, peeled and shredded

2 teaspoons grated orange rind

1 small leek, sliced

1 red pepper, cored, deseeded and sliced

50 g (2 oz) water chestnuts, drained and sliced

50 g (2 oz) bean sprouts

Sauce:

6 tablespoons vegetable or chicken stock

6 tablespoons fresh orange juice

2 tablespoons dark soy sauce

1 tablespoon rice or wine vinegar

2 teaspoons clear honey

pepper

Serves 4

Preparation time: 10 minutes, plus marinating

Cooking time: 10 minutes

rapid-fried prawns

1 Wash and trim the prawns, removing the legs but leaving the tail pieces firmly attached. Remove the black intestinal vein and pat dry with kitchen paper. Heat the oil in a deep wok until it is very hot. Turn down the heat to allow the oil to cool a little, then deep-fry the prawns until they turn bright pink. Remove them with a slotted spoon and dry on kitchen paper.

2 Pour off all but 1 tablespoon of oil from the wok and increase the heat to high. Quickly mix together the sauce ingredients and add to the wok with the prawns. Cook for about 1 minute, stirring.

3 Mix the cornflour to a smooth paste with the measured water. Add to the wok and stir until all the prawns are coated with the sauce.

500 g (1 lb) headless uncooked prawns

vegetable oil, for deep-frying

2 teaspoons cornflour

1 tablespoon cold water

Sweet and Sour Sauce:

2 tablespoons dry sherry

2 tablespoons soy sauce

2 tablespoons vinegar

1 tablespoon sugar

1 teaspoon finely chopped spring onion

1 teaspoon finely chopped fresh root ginger

Serves 4

Preparation time: 10 minutes

Cooking time: 5 minutes

chinese fried noodles

1 Fill a large saucepan with water, add salt and bring to the boil. Add the egg noodles and cook until tender but still firm. Drain in a colander then rinse under cold running water until cool. Set aside.

2 Heat about 3 tablespoons of the oil in a hot wok or frying pan. Add the onion, shredded meat, mangetout and bean sprouts and stir-fry for 1 minute. Add 1 teaspoon of salt and stir a few more times. Remove the meat and vegetables from the wok using a slotted spoon and keep warm.

3 Heat the remaining oil in the wok and add the spring onions, drained noodles and about half the stir-fried meat and vegetable mixture. Mix in the soy sauce and stir-fry for 1–2 minutes, or until heated through. Transfer the mixture to a warmed serving dish and pour the remaining stir-fried meat and vegetable mixture over the top. Sprinkle with sesame oil or chilli sauce and serve immediately.

500 g (1 lb) egg noodles

4 tablespoons vegetable oil

1 onion, thinly sliced

125 g (4 oz) cooked meat, e.g. pork, chicken or ham, shredded

125 g (4 oz) mangetout, trimmed

125 g (4 oz) bean sprouts

2–3 spring onions, thinly shredded

2 tablespoons light soy sauce

salt

1 tablespoon sesame oil or chilli sauce, to finish

Serves 3–4

Preparation time: 15 minutes

Cooking time: 10 minutes

1 Heat the oil in a heavy-based saucepan, add the onion and garlic and cook over a gentle heat, stirring frequently, for about 4 minutes or until softened. Stir in the mild curry paste and cook for a further 2 minutes.

2 Add the coconut milk and lime juice to the pan, stir to mix and simmer for 3 minutes. Add the ground almonds, prawns and salt to taste, then simmer the curry gently for a further 3 minutes until all the prawns have turned pink and the curry sauce has thickened slightly.

3 Stir the diced mango into the curry and heat through for 1 minute. Taste and adjust the seasoning if necessary. Transfer the curry to a serving dish, scatter the chopped coriander over the top and serve immediately.

2 tablespoons groundnut oil

1 red onion, finely chopped

2 garlic cloves, crushed

4 tablespoons mild curry paste

400 ml (14 fl oz) coconut milk

juice of 1 lime

2 tablespoons ground almonds

24 uncooked peeled prawns

1 small ripe mango, peeled and diced

salt

2 tablespoons coarsely chopped coriander, to garnish

Serves 4

Preparation time: 10 minutes

Cooking time: 15 minutes

prawn & mango curry

thai red beef curry

1   Heat the oil in a heavy-based saucepan and add the curry paste, ground coriander and cumin and the lime leaves. Cook over a gentle heat, stirring frequently, for 3 minutes.

2   Add the beef strips to the pan, mix to coat them evenly in the curry paste and cook gently, stirring frequently, for a further 5 minutes.

3   Add 200 ml (7 fl oz) of the coconut milk to the pan, stir to combine and simmer gently for 5 minutes until most of the coconut milk has been absorbed. Stir in the remaining coconut milk with the peanut butter, fish sauce and sugar. Simmer gently for a further 5 minutes, until the sauce is thick and the beef is tender. Garnish with coriander sprigs, and serve immediately with steamed rice.

3 tablespoons groundnut oil

3 tablespoons Thai red curry paste

½ teaspoon ground coriander

½ teaspoon ground cumin

4 Kaffir lime leaves, shredded

500 g (1 lb) beef fillet, cut into thin strips

400 ml (14 fl oz) coconut milk

2 tablespoons crunchy peanut butter

2 teaspoons fish sauce (nam pla)

1 tablespoon soft brown sugar

coriander sprigs, to garnish

Serves 4

Preparation time: 5–10 minutes

Cooking time: 20 minutes

simple beef curry with spinach

1 Heat the ghee or oil in a pan, add the onion and garlic and fry over a gentle heat, stirring frequently, for about 5 minutes until softened but not coloured. Stir in the chillies and fry for a further 2 minutes. Add the cloves, garam masala, coriander, turmeric, chilli powder and cumin. Stir well to mix and fry, stirring constantly, for 2 minutes.

2 Stir in the beef and salt and cook, stirring, for 3 minutes to seal the meat, then add the tomatoes, coconut milk and spinach and stir to mix. Cover the pan and simmer the curry gently, stirring occasionally, for 20 minutes.

3 Stir in the lemon juice and cook the curry, uncovered, for a further 8–10 minutes, stirring occasionally, until the sauce has thickened. Taste and adjust the seasoning if necessary and serve immediately.

2 tablespoons ghee or vegetable oil

1 large onion, thinly sliced

2 garlic cloves, crushed

2 green chillies, deseeded and sliced

2 whole cloves, bruised

1 teaspoon garam masala

1 teaspoon ground coriander

1 teaspoon turmeric

½ teaspoon chilli powder

1½ teaspoons ground cumin

625 g (1¼ lb) beef fillet, cut into bite-sized pieces

1 teaspoon salt

175 g (6 oz) tomatoes, cut into large dice

150 ml (¼ pint) coconut milk

250 g (8 oz) ready-washed young leaf spinach

1 teaspoon lemon juice

Serves 4

Preparation time: 20 minutes

Cooking time: 35–40 minutes

■ If you would like to make this curry hotter, add some of the chilli seeds to it. Saffron rice would be a good accompaniment.

sardines with herb sauce •

cod steaks with parsley butter •

griddled salmon fillets with pesto & lemon rice •

barbecued duck breasts •

spiced country chicken •

baked tarragon chicken •

chicken cordon bleu •

chicory & smoked bacon gratin •

liver & bacon with roasted tomato chutney •

rare roast beef with tomatoes & mustard relish •

lamb chops with chutney •

honey-glazed lamb chops •

pork fillet with herbs •

meat & fish dishes

8 sardines, scaled and cleaned

40 g (1½ oz) parsley leaves

20 g (¾ oz) fresh mixed herbs, (e.g. basil, chives, mint)

1 garlic clove, chopped

1 tablespoon capers, drained and washed

2 canned anchovy fillets in oil, drained and chopped

1 teaspoon Dijon mustard

125 ml (4 fl oz) extra virgin olive oil

salt and pepper

lime wedges, to serve

basil sprigs, to garnish

1 Preheat a barbecue or a grill. If using a grill, place the sardines on an oiled grill pan.

2 Place all the remaining ingredients in a food processor or blender with 2 tablespoons of warm water and blend to a smooth paste. Season to taste.

3 Spread a little of the sauce over the fish and barbecue or grill for 3 minutes. Turn the fish over, spread with a little more sauce and grill for a further 3 minutes, until the sardines are cooked. Serve immediately with extra herb sauce, lime wedges and sprigs of basil.

Serves 4
Preparation time: 10 minutes
Cooking time: 6 minutes

sardines with herb sauce

cod steaks with parsley butter

1 Season the fish generously with salt and pepper on each side. Cover and chill while preparing the parsley butter.

2 Beat the butter until soft and creamy. Work in the parsley, lemon juice and seasoning to taste. Using half the butter, spread a little over each side of each fish steak.

3 Place the cod steaks on a sheet of foil and cook under a pre-heated moderate grill for 6–8 minutes on each side or until the fish is cooked through. Top with the remaining parsley butter and garnish with lemon wedges and a coriander sprig, if liked. Serve immediately.

4 cod steaks

125 g (4 oz) butter

1 tablespoon chopped parsley

1 tablespoon lemon juice

salt and pepper

To Garnish:

lemon wedges

coriander sprig (optional)

Serves 4

Preparation time: 10 minutes

Cooking time: 12–16 minutes

griddled salmon fillets with pesto & lemon rice

1 Bring a large saucepan of water to the boil, add the rice and the lemon rind and return to the boil. Simmer gently for 10–12 minutes until the rice is cooked. Meanwhile, to make the pesto, place all the ingredients in a food processor or blender and process until smooth or blend with a mortar and pestle.

2 Heat a griddle pan. Remove any bones from the salmon with a pair of tweezers and pat the salmon dry with kitchen paper. Place the fillets on the hot griddle, skin side down, and cook for 3 minutes. Turn and cook for another 2–3 minutes until cooked through and firm to the touch.

3 Drain the rice and immediately stir in the lemon juice and butter. Season to taste. Serve the salmon fillets on a bed of rice with the pesto sauce. Garnish with basil leaves, if liked.

75 g (3 oz) long-grain rice

grated rind and juice of 1 lemon

4 salmon fillets, 150 g (5 oz) each

50 g (2 oz) butter

basil leaves, to garnish (optional)

Pesto:

1 garlic clove, chopped

15 g (½ oz) basil leaves

15 g (½ oz) pine nuts

3 tablespoons extra virgin olive oil

1 tablespoon freshly grated Parmesan cheese

sea salt flakes and pepper

Serves 4
Preparation time: 5 minutes
Cooking time: about 20 minutes

barbecued duck breasts

1 Mix all the marinade ingredients together in a small jug. Score the skin of the duck breasts, place them in a shallow dish and pour the marinade over them. Cover and leave to marinate in a cool place for at least 4 hours.

2 Drain the duck breasts and reserve the marinade. Cook under a preheated grill for about 2 minutes on each side to extract most of the fat and to avoid any flare-up on the barbecue.

3 Place the duck breasts on the oiled grill of a preheated barbecue and cook for 2–6 minutes on each side, according to taste, basting frequently with the reserved marinade. Garnish with chervil sprigs and serve with a colourful mixed salad.

4 duck breasts, about 175 g (6 oz) each

chervil sprigs, to garnish

Marinade:

finely grated rind and juice of 1 orange

1 tablespoon dark soy sauce

3 teaspoons clear honey

1 cm (½ inch) piece of fresh root ginger, peeled and finely chopped

salt and pepper

Serves 4

Preparation time: 15 minutes, plus marinating

Cooking time: 8–16 minutes

4 chicken portions

2 tablespoons plain flour

25 g (1 oz) butter

1 onion, finely chopped

1 garlic clove, crushed

1 green pepper, cored, deseeded and chopped

2 teaspoons curry powder

1 teaspoon chopped thyme

250 g (8 oz) can tomatoes

2 tablespoons dry white vermouth

50 g (2 oz) raisins

salt and pepper

Serves 4

Preparation time: 10 minutes

Cooking time: 35 minutes

1 Coat the chicken portions with flour. Melt the butter in a large pan, add the chicken and fry briskly until golden all over. Remove from the pan and set aside.

2 Add the onion, garlic, green pepper, curry powder and thyme to the fat remaining in the pan and fry, stirring, for 5 minutes.

3 Add the tomatoes with their juice and the vermouth. Return the chicken to the pan and add salt and pepper to taste. Cover and cook for 20 minutes, or until the chicken is tender. Stir in the raisins and serve hot, with jacket potatoes or plain boiled rice.

spiced country chicken

baked tarragon chicken

1 Place the chicken breasts on a baking sheet, drizzle on each side with a little oil and place in a preheated oven, 230°C (450°F), Gas Mark 8, for 20 minutes, turning them over after 10 minutes.

2 While the chicken breasts are cooking, melt the butter and the oil in a large frying pan until the fat begins to sizzle. Stir in the flour and cook for 1 minute. Stir in the orange juice with the water. Add the tarragon, garlic and salt and pepper and slowly bring to the boil, stirring constantly until the sauce is thick and smooth.

3 Using a spatula, transfer the chicken breasts to warmed plates, pour sauce over each piece of chicken and garnish with orange and tarragon. Serve immediately.

■ Variation: Substitute dry white wine for the orange juice and thyme for the tarragon.

4 boneless, skinless chicken breasts

oil, for drizzling

1 tablespoon butter

1 tablespoon oil

1 teaspoon plain flour

150 ml (¼ pint) frozen concentrated Jaffa orange juice, thawed

2–3 tablespoons water

1 teaspoon chopped tarragon or a pinch of dried tarragon

1 garlic clove, crushed

salt and pepper

To Garnish:

1 orange, peeled and cut into rings

tarragon sprigs

Serves 4
Preparation time: 5 minutes
Cooking time: 20 minutes

chicken cordon bleu

1 Dry the chicken breasts well, then slit them to make a 'pocket'. Insert the slices of ham and cheese into the pockets.

2 Mix a little salt and pepper with the flour. Dust the chicken breasts with the seasoned flour, then coat in beaten egg and finally bread-crumbs. Fry in preheated hot oil until crisp, golden brown and tender – about 12–15 minutes. Garnish with parsley sprigs and serve with salad.

4 boneless, skinless chicken breasts

4 slices of ham

4 slices of Gruyère cheese

15 g (½ oz) flour

1 egg, beaten

50 g (2 oz) soft breadcrumbs

oil, for frying

salt and pepper

parsley sprigs, to garnish

Serves 4
Preparation time: 5 minutes
Cooking time: 12–15 minutes

■ Variation: For Chicken Rossini, fill the chicken breasts with pâté and finely diced uncooked mushrooms instead of ham and cheese. Coat and fry as above.

chicory & smoked bacon gratin

1 Place the bacon in a nonstick frying pan and fry in its own fat until crisp. Meanwhile, trim a thin slice from the root end of the chicory, if discoloured, and remove any damaged or brown leaves. If it is just the tips of the leaves that have developed a brown edge, trim them with scissors. Cut each chicory head in half lengthways and remove the central core, leaving the head intact.

2 Melt the butter in a large frying pan, add the chicory cut-side down and sprinkle with the lemon juice. Fry until browning, turning several times and taking care to keep the heads together.

3 Transfer the chicory to a 2–2.5 litre (3½–4 pint) gratin dish and scatter with the fried bacon. Mix together the mustard, cream and two-thirds of the cheese, season with salt and pepper and pour over the chicory. Scatter the remaining cheese over the top and place in a preheated oven, 200–225°C (400–425°F), Gas Mark 6–7, for about 20 minutes until bubbling and golden. Finish the browning under a hot grill, if necessary. Garnish with chervil sprigs and serve.

8 large, thin, lightly smoked bacon rashers, rinded and chopped

8 chicory heads

25 g (1 oz) butter

juice of 1 large lemon

2 tablespoons Dijon mustard

300 ml (½ pint) single cream

150 g (5 oz) Gruyère or mature Cheddar cheese, grated

salt and pepper

chervil sprigs, to garnish

Serves 4
Preparation time: 15 minutes
Cooking time: 30 minutes

■ Witloof chicory has a slightly bitter taste and delicately wilted texture when cooked. It combines beautifully with rich creamy sauces and sharp, piquant flavours such as lemon and orange juice, olives, capers and anchovies.

liver & bacon with roasted tomato chutney

1 Spoon 2 tablespoons of the olive oil into a roasting tin and place in a preheated oven, 220° (425°F), Gas Mark 7. Add the tomatoes, turn them in the oil to coat well and place the tin at the top of the oven. Roast for 40 minutes, or until the tomatoes begin to darken around the edges.

2 Heat the remaining tablespoon of olive oil in a frying pan and add the onion and garlic. Fry over a low heat for 5 minutes, then add the raisins, brown sugar, vinegar, rosemary, mustard seeds and salt and pepper. Mix well and simmer for 2 minutes. Mix in the roasted tomatoes, then remove from the heat.

3 Heat a griddle pan and cook the bacon until crispy, about 2 minutes on each side. Keep warm. Place the calves' liver on the griddle and cook for 2 minutes on each side for pink, or 4 minutes for well done. Serve at once with the bacon and roasted tomato chutney, garnished with rosemary sprigs.

■ Make more chutney if you wish and store it in the refrigerator for up to 2–3 weeks to serve with any cold meats. If time is very short, serve a good ready-made chutney instead.

3 tablespoons olive oil

750 g (1½ lb) tomatoes, halved and green cores removed

1 red onion, sliced

1 garlic clove, crushed and chopped

50 g (2 oz) raisins

50 g (2 oz) brown sugar

3 tablespoons white wine vinegar

1 teaspoon chopped rosemary

1 teaspoon black mustard seeds

8 smoked streaky bacon rashers, rinded

4 slices of calves' liver, about 125 g (4 oz) each

sea salt flakes and pepper

rosemary sprigs, to garnish

Serves 4

Preparation time: 10 minutes

Cooking time: about 55 minutes

rare roast beef with tomatoes & mustard relish

1 Heat a griddle pan. Season the beef fillet with salt and pepper and pat in the seasoning. Place on the griddle and cook for 4 minutes on all sides until charred on the outside, about 20–25 minutes.

2 Transfer the beef fillet to a lightly oiled roasting tin and place in a preheated oven, 220°C (425°F), Gas Mark 7, for 10–15 minutes for rare and 20–25 minutes for medium. Remove from the oven and allow to rest for 10 minutes.

3 Heat the oil in a frying pan. Add the garlic and onions and cook for 5 minutes. Add the tomatoes, season and warm through for 3 minutes.

4 Warm the two mustards in a small saucepan with the honey. Stir until blended. Add the coriander to the tomato mixture. Slice the beef fillet and serve on a bed of the tomato mixture, with the mustard sauce drizzled over the top.

1.25 kg (2½ lb) beef fillet

1 tablespoon olive oil, plus extra for oiling

1 garlic clove, sliced

2 red onions, sliced

16 small tomatoes

2 tablespoons Dijon mustard

2 tablespoons coarse grain mustard

2 tablespoons clear honey

2 tablespoons chopped coriander

sea salt flakes and pepper

Serves 8
Preparation time: 20 minutes
Cooking time: 50 minutes

lamb chops with chutney

1 To make the marinade, mix together all the ingredients and place in a shallow dish. Rub the chops with the marinade, cover and leave to marinate for 1 hour, turning from time to time.

2 To make the coriander chutney, place all the ingredients in a food processor or blender and blend until smooth. Stop the machine every so often and push down any bits with a spatula and blend again. Turn into a small bowl to serve.

3 Place each lamb chop on a skewer. Pull the onion wedges apart and thread a few pieces on to each skewer with the chop. Season with a little salt, place under a preheated hot grill and cook for 4–5 minutes on each side. Serve with the chutney and a green salad.

4 lamb loin chops

1 red onion, cut into 8 wedges

½ teaspoon salt

Marinade:

2 garlic cloves, crushed

2.5 cm (1 inch) piece of fresh root ginger, crushed in a garlic press

2 tablespoons sunflower or vegetable oil

2 teaspoons ground coriander

1 teaspoon ground cumin

½ teaspoon ground cloves

¼ teaspoon ground cinnamon

¼ teaspoon pepper

Coriander Chutney:

8 tablespoons chopped coriander leaves

1 small green chilli, deseeded and finely chopped

1 teaspoon garam masala

1 teaspoon sugar

1 teaspoon salt

2 tablespoons lime or lemon juice

Serves 4

Preparation time: 5 minutes, plus marinating

Cooking time: 8–10 minutes

honey-glazed lamb chops

1 Season the chops well. Beat the butter or margarine until pale and creamy then blend in the honey, mustard and seasoning to taste to form a smooth paste. Brush the honey mixture over the chops, then cover and chill for about 1 hour.

2 Grill the chops under a preheated hot grill for 5 minutes on each side. Serve garnished with a little chopped parsley and sprigs of watercress and accompanied by broccoli and jacket potatoes.

4 lamb chump chops

50 g (2 oz) butter or margarine

2 tablespoons clear honey

2 teaspoons wholegrain mustard

salt and pepper

To Garnish:

chopped parsley

watercress sprigs

Serves 4

Preparation time: 10 minutes, plus marinating

Cooking time: 10 minutes

1 tablespoon soya or sunflower oil

4 shallots or small onions, finely chopped

1 garlic clove, crushed and chopped

1 Heat the oil in a small saucepan, add the shallots and garlic and cook gently for 3 minutes, but do not allow to brown. Sprinkle in the flour and stir. Stir in the wine, cook gently until the sauce is smooth and season to taste with salt and pepper.

1 tablespoon wholemeal flour

150 ml (¼ pint) dry white wine

750 g (1½ lb) pork fillet, thinly sliced

125 g (4 oz) broccoli florets

2 tablespoons chopped sage leaves

2 tablespoons chopped chives

2 Heat a griddle pan and add the sliced pork fillet in batches. Cook each batch for 3 minutes on each side and keep warm. Meanwhile, blanch the broccoli in a small saucepan of boiling water for 1 minute, drain, then add to the sauce.

2 tablespoons chopped thyme

50 g (2 oz) pistachio nuts, shelled and chopped

1 orange pepper, cored, deseeded and sliced (optional)

sea salt flakes and pepper

lemon wedges, to garnish

3 Add the herbs and pistachio nuts and orange pepper, if using, to the sauce and heat through, stirring, for 1 minute. Serve the pork with the sauce and garnish with lemon wedges.

Serves 4–6
Preparation time: 20 minutes
Cooking time: 15–20 minutes

pork fillet with herbs

warm duck & orange salad •

warm chorizo salad •

king prawn & bacon salad •

french bean salad with ham •

classic french dressing •

pasta with goats' cheese •

sweet pepper dressing •

pasta, pea & artichoke salad •

caesar salad •

herb salad with grilled haloumi •

mozzarella salad with pesto •

classic potato salad •

potato & broad bean salad •

salads

warm duck & orange salad

1 Using a sharp knife, make 4 diagonal slashes in the skin of each duck breast. Season with salt and pepper, rubbing the mixture into the skin and flesh.

2 Heat both the oils in a large frying pan. Add the duck breasts and cook over a fairly high heat for 5–7 minutes, turning once, until well browned on the outside but still rosy pink on the inside. Using tongs, transfer the duck breasts to a plate and keep warm.

3 Add the courgettes to the oil remaining in the pan and stir in the garlic, if using. Cook, stirring, for 1–2 minutes, until the courgettes have started to soften. Using a slotted spoon, transfer the courgettes to a bowl. Add the orange segments to the sliced courgettes.

4 To make the dressing, stir all the ingredients together in a small bowl or place them in a screw-top jar and shake well to combine. Arrange the salad leaves on 4 individual plates. Slice the duck breasts and arrange the slices next to the leaves, with portions of the courgette and orange salad next to the duck. Spoon the dressing over the salad and serve it warm, garnished with the sesame seeds and orange rind. Serve with a green salad.

2 boneless duck breasts

1 tablespoon olive oil

2 teaspoons sesame oil

2 courgettes, sliced

1 garlic clove, chopped (optional)

2 small oranges, peeled and segmented

about 250 g (8 oz) salad leaves (e.g. chicory, rocket, spinach, lollo rosso)

salt and pepper

Dressing:

4 tablespoons olive oil

1 teaspoon sesame oil

1 tablespoon red wine vinegar

1 teaspoon grated orange rind

1 teaspoon finely chopped parsley

pinch of dried sage

To Garnish:

toasted sesame seeds

long strips of orange rind

Serves 4
Preparation time: 20 minutes
Cooking time: 6–9 minutes

1 Arrange the salad leaves on individual plates, or tear the leaves into bite-sized pieces and place in a large salad bowl. Scatter the sage leaves over them.

2 Heat the olive oil in a frying pan until fairly hot. Add the sliced chorizo sausage and fry over a high heat for 1 minute. Add the onion and garlic and fry for 1–2 minutes more, or until the chorizo is browned. Remove the pan from the heat.

3 Stir the vinegar into the pan, with salt and pepper to taste. Quickly spoon the mixture over the salad leaves and toss lightly. Serve at once.

about 250 g (8 oz) salad leaves (e.g. radicchio, chicory, frisé)

small handful of sage leaves

5 tablespoons extra virgin olive oil

300 g (10 oz) chorizo sausage, skinned and thinly sliced

1 small red onion, thinly sliced

1 garlic clove, chopped

2 tablespoons red wine vinegar

salt and pepper

Serves 4

Preparation time: 15 minutes

Cooking time: 2–3 minutes

warm chorizo salad

1 Add the sugar snap peas to a saucepan of boiling water and cook for 1 minute, then drain in a colander and cool under cold running water. Drain thoroughly and place in a large bowl with the spring onions.

2 Cut the bacon rashers in half and wrap a half rasher around each prawn. Place on a rack over a foil-lined grill pan and cook under a preheated medium-hot grill for about 4 minutes, turning once, until the bacon is crisp and the prawns are hot.

3 While the prawns are cooking, arrange the mixed salad leaves on 4 individual serving plates. Add the cooked prawns and any cooking juices from the grill pan to the sugar snap peas and spring onions. Pour the dressing over and season with salt and pepper. (Go easy on the salt as the bacon and prawns are naturally salty.) Toss gently to mix all the ingredients together. Arrange the prawns and vegetables on top of the salad leaves and serve at once.

250 g (8 oz) sugar snap peas or mangetout

2 spring onions, shredded

6 smoky streaky bacon rashers, rinds removed

12 cooked Mediterranean (king) prawns, peeled

about 250 g (8 oz) mixed salad leaves (e.g. red oakleaf, watercress, lamb's lettuce, four seasons, rocket)

Classic French Dressing (see page 69)

salt and pepper

Serves 4
Preparation time: 15 minutes
Cooking time: 5 minutes

king prawn & bacon salad

french bean salad with ham

1 Bring a saucepan of water to the boil, add the beans and cook for 2–3 minutes, or until just tender. Drain in a colander, refresh under cold running water and drain again. Blot the excess water with kitchen paper and place the beans in a serving bowl.

2 Using 2 forks, shred the ham. Add to the beans with the spring onions, parsley, salt and pepper.

3 Pour the French dressing over the salad and toss lightly. Serve from the bowl or arrange on 4 individual plates. Garnish with a few salad or parsley leaves.

375 g (12 oz) French beans, topped and tailed

250 g (8 oz) cooked ham

4 spring onions, finely chopped

2 tablespoons chopped parsley

1 quantity Classic French Dressing

salt and pepper

salad or parsley leaves, to garnish

Serves 4
Preparation time: 15 minutes
Cooking time: 2–3 minutes

classic french dressing

1 Combine the vinegar, garlic, mustard and sugar in a small bowl. Add salt and pepper to taste and stir thoroughly.

2 Gradually whisk in the olive oil. Taste and add more salt and pepper, if necessary.

3 Alternatively, put all the ingredients in a screw-top jar, close the lid tightly and shake well until combined. Use as required.

2 tablespoons red or white wine vinegar

1–2 garlic cloves, crushed

2 teaspoons Dijon mustard

¼ teaspoon caster sugar

6 tablespoons olive oil

salt and pepper

Makes about 150 ml (¼ pint)
Preparation time: 5 minutes

pasta with goats' cheese

1 Add the pasta shells to a large saucepan of boiling salted water and cook until tender. Drain in a colander and rinse under cold running water to cool. Drain thoroughly on kitchen paper.

2 Meanwhile, place the peeled prawns in a bowl with the goats' cheese and the spring onions. Add the lemon juice and season with salt and pepper. Mix together gently.

3 Use the prawn mixture to stuff the pasta shells. Serve 2 shells per person on individual plates in a pool of sweet pepper dressing. Serve garnished with fresh herbs.

8 giant pasta shells

500 g (1 lb) cooked peeled prawns

175 g (6 oz) soft young goats' cheese

4 spring onions, finely chopped

1 teaspoon lemon juice

1 quantity Sweet Pepper Dressing

salt and pepper

fresh herbs, to garnish

Serves 4
Preparation time: 15 minutes
Cooking time: 12–14 minutes

sweet pepper dressing

1 Cook the peppers under a preheated hot grill for 15–20 minutes, turning occasionally, until the skin is blistered and blackened all over. Transfer to a bowl, cover with layers of kitchen paper and set aside.

2 When cool enough to handle, rub off and discard the charred skins. Cut each pepper in half and remove the seeds. Roughly chop the flesh.

3 Place the grilled pepper flesh in a blender or food processor. Add the garlic, paprika, mustard and vinegar, with salt and pepper to taste. Process until fairly smooth. With the motor running slowly, carefully pour in the oil until the dressing is smooth. Adjust the seasoning to taste.

2 red peppers

1 garlic clove, crushed

1 teaspoon paprika

½ teaspoon mustard powder

4 teaspoons red wine vinegar

125 ml (4 fl oz) light olive oil

salt and pepper

Makes 300 ml (½ pint)
Preparation time: 5 minutes
Cooking time: 15–20 minutes

■ You can use peppers of any colour, but red peppers give a vibrant tone.

pasta, pea & artichoke salad

1 Cook the pasta in plenty of boiling lightly salted water until tender. Drain well.

2 Turn the pasta into a large salad bowl and add the artichoke hearts, peas and pimiento. Sprinkle with the nutmeg, season with salt and pepper and turn gently with two forks, making sure the pasta does not break up.

3 Combine all the dressing ingredients in a jug, whisking with a fork until smooth, then pour over the salad and fork through lightly to coat all the ingredients with dressing. Serve the salad at room temperature, on its own or as an accompaniment to grilled fish or veal.

250 g (8 oz) coloured pasta bows or shells

400 g (13 oz) can artichoke hearts, drained and sliced

475 g (15 oz) petis pois, defrosted if frozen

1 canned sweet pimiento, drained and diced

½ teaspoon freshly grated nutmeg

salt and pepper

Dressing:

1 tablespoon white vermouth

1 tablespoon lemon juice

3 tablespoons olive oil

4 tablespoons soured cream

Serves 4

Preparation time: 5 minutes

Cooking time: about 10 minutes

caesar salad

1 To make the dressing, put the mayonnaise in a bowl and stir in enough water to make a thin, pourable sauce. Crush the garlic to a paste with a little salt. Add to the mayonnaise with the Parmesan and stir. Thin with more water, if necessary, so the sauce remains pourable. Add pepper to taste.

2 Tear the lettuce leaves into large pieces and place in a shallow salad bowl. Snip the anchovies into small pieces and scatter over the lettuce leaves.

3 To make croûtons, cut the bread into 3 cm (1¼ inch) thick slices and remove the crusts. Dip a brush into the melted butter and butter the slices of bread. Cut into 3 cm (1¼ inch) cubes. Brush a baking sheet with some butter. Arrange the bread cubes on it, brushing the cut sides with any remaining butter. Place in a preheated oven, 200°C (400°F), Gas Mark 6, for about 12 minutes, or until crisp and golden. Watch the croûtons carefully after 8 minutes, as they tend to colour quickly towards the end of the cooking time and may burn.

4 To serve, add the hot croûtons to the salad bowl and drizzle the dressing over the top. Sprinkle the Parmesan over and serve.

1 cos lettuce, separated into leaves

50 g (2 oz) can anchovies in olive oil, drained

1 small rustic white loaf (unsliced)

75 g (3 oz) butter, melted

3 tablespoons freshly grated Parmesan cheese

Dressing:

5 tablespoons mayonnaise

4–5 tablespoons water

1–2 garlic cloves

3 tablespoons finely chopped Parmesan cheese

coarse sea salt and pepper

Serves 4–6

Preparation time: 20 minutes

Cooking time: about 12 minutes

herb salad with grilled haloumi

1 Tear the lettuce into bite-sized pieces and place in a large, shallow salad bowl with the rocket or leaf spinach and mixed herbs.

2 Cut the haloumi cheese into small cubes of less than 2.5 cm (1 inch). Place these in a baking tin large enough to hold them in one layer. Add the olive oil and season with pepper. Toss gently to coat the cheese and heat under a preheated hot grill, stirring occasionally, for about 8 minutes until golden brown on all sides. Scatter over the salad leaves.

3 Add the French dressing to the salad and toss well. Serve the salad immediately.

1 cos lettuce

about 50 g (2 oz) rocket or young leaf spinach

handful of mixed herbs, roughly torn (e.g. dill, chervil, coriander, basil, parsley)

250 g (8 oz) haloumi cheese

1–2 tablespoons olive oil

½ quantity Classic French Dressing (see page 69)

pepper

Serves 6–8
Preparation time: 20 minutes
Cooking time: about 8 minutes

■ Haloumi is superb for grilling or frying as it develops a golden crust and does not melt. It is readily available in large super-markets or Cypriot stores.

mozzarella salad
with pesto

1 Tear the salad leaves into bite-sized pieces and arrange on a platter or shallow serving dish. Scatter the bocconcini or diced mozzarella over the leaves and sprinkle with the red onion. Add salt and pepper to taste.

2 Spoon the dressing over the bocconcini or mozzarella and garnish the salad with the fresh basil leaves and oregano sprigs.

■ To make a pesto dressing, dilute the pesto sauce on page 50 with 2 tablespoons of white wine vinegar and a little more olive oil if required.

1 cos or other crisp green lettuce, separated into leaves

1 small head of frisé

250 g (8 oz) bocconcini or diced mozzarella

1 red onion, chopped

salt and pepper

½ quantity Pesto Dressing (see left)

To Garnish:

basil leaves

oregano sprigs

| **Serves 4** |
| **Preparation time:** 10 minutes |

classic potato salad

1 Cook the potatoes, whole and in their skins, in a large pan of boiling water for about 15 minutes, or until tender. Drain and refresh under cold running water, then drain thoroughly and allow to cool.

2 Slice the potatoes thickly and place in a serving bowl with the chopped spring onions. Add salt and pepper to taste.

3 To make the dressing, stir together the mayonnaise, cream and mustard. Spoon the dressing over the salad and toss lightly to mix. Serve the salad sprinkled with the chives.

750 g (1½ lb) waxy salad potatoes

4 spring onions, finely chopped

salt and pepper

2 tablespoons snipped chives, to garnish

Dressing:

6 tablespoons mayonnaise

3 tablespoons single cream

1 teaspoon Dijon mustard

Serves 6
Preparation time: 15 minutes
Cooking time: about 15 minutes

■ Choose potato varieties with a waxy texture, such as Charlotte or Pink Fir Apple. They will retain their shape better than floury baking potatoes.

potato & broad bean salad

1 Cook the potatoes in a saucepan of salted boiling water for about 10–15 minutes until they are just tender. Drain well. Cook the broad beans in a saucepan of lightly salted boiling water until just tender. Drain.

2 Cut the warm potatoes into quarters and place in a bowl. Combine the dressing and the mayonnaise in a jug and season well with salt and pepper. Pour the mixture over the potatoes and toss until coated.

3 Add the beans, pepperoni, spring onions and olives or pickled walnuts: toss again. Spoon the salad into a bowl. Cover and chill in the refrigerator until required.

750 g (1½ lb) new potatoes, scrubbed

375 g (12 oz) frozen broad beans

75 ml (3 fl oz) Classic French Dressing (see page 69)

150 ml (¼ pint) thick mayonnaise

75 g (3 oz) pepperoni, sliced

1 bunch spring onions, finely sliced

125 g (4 oz) black olives or drained pickled walnuts, quartered

salt and pepper

Serves 6–8

Preparation time: 15 minutes, plus chilling

Cooking time: 10–15 minutes

chocolate pancake stack with rum butter ●

crunchy banana & pineapple pie ●

pineapple & apricot fritters ●

poached figs ●

blueberry kissel ●

cranachan with fruit kissel ●

lemon syllabub ●

champagne syllabub & strawberries ●

pots au chocolat ●

cinnamon & apple pudding ●

strawberry crumble flan ●

white chocolate soufflés ●

chocolate rum truffles ●

almond petits fours ●

sweet things

chocolate pancake stack with rum butter

1 To make the rum butter, beat the butter in a bowl until soft. Add the icing sugar and the rum and beat together until light and creamy. Transfer to a serving dish.

2 To make the pancakes, sift the flour, cocoa powder and baking powder into a bowl. Add the sugar. Make a well in the centre, then add the egg and a little of the milk. Whisk the mixture to make a stiff batter, then beat in the remaining milk. Stir in the chocolate, sultanas and almonds.

3 Heat a little oil in a large frying pan or griddle. Take spoonfuls of the batter, making sure you scoop up some fruit, nuts and chocolate each time, and spoon into the pan. Fry gently until just firm and browned on the underside. Turn the pancakes and cook for a further 1 minute. Drain and keep warm while cooking the remainder. Stack the pancakes and top with spoonfuls of the rum butter.

■ There are many simple variations to this recipe; white or plain chocolate, grated orange or walnuts are equally good in the pancakes, while brandy or an orange-flavoured liqueur can be used instead of rum in the butter.

Rum Butter:

75 g (3 oz) unsalted butter, softened

50 g (2 oz) icing sugar

3 tablespoons rum

Pancakes:

100 g (3½ oz) self-raising flour

15 g (½ oz) cocoa powder

½ teaspoon baking powder

25 g (1 oz) caster sugar

1 egg

175 ml (6 fl oz) milk

125 g (4 oz) milk chocolate, roughly chopped

25 g (1 oz) sultanas

25 g (1 oz) slivered or flaked almonds

oil, for shallow frying

Serves 4–6

Preparation time: 15 minutes

Cooking time: 12–15 minutes

crunchy banana & pineapple pie

1 Crumb the biscuits in a food processor or place them between 2 large sheets of greaseproof paper and crush with a rolling pin. Melt the butter in a saucepan, add the crumbs and stir well. Place 3 tablespoons of the crumb mixture in a small ovenproof dish. Press the remainder over the base and sides of a buttered 20 cm (8 inch) pie plate.

2 Bake the pie case and crumbs in a preheated oven, 200°C (400°F), Gas Mark 6, for 10 minutes until crisp, then leave to cool.

3 Mash the banana with half the pineapple, then mix in the cheese, sugar and vanilla. Spread the mixture over the pie case. Pile the reserved pineapple on top and sprinkle with the baked crumbs. Chill until ready to serve.

175 g (6 oz) ginger biscuits

75 g (3 oz) butter

1 banana

200 g (7 oz) pineapple chunks, drained if using canned pineapple

375 g (12 oz) medium-fat soft cheese

75 g (3 oz) caster sugar

1 teaspoon vanilla extract

Serves 6–8

Preparation time: 15 minutes

Cooking time: 10 minutes

pineapple & apricot fritters

1 Drain the pineapple rings and apricot halves, pat dry with kitchen paper and dust with flour.

2 To make the batter, sift the flour, mixed spice and salt into a bowl. Gradually beat in the egg yolk, water and oil to form a smooth batter. Whisk the egg white until stiff and fold into the batter.

3 Heat the oil for deep-frying to 180°C (350°F), or until a cube of stale bread dropped in browns in 30 seconds. Dip the pieces of fruit into the batter to coat well and fry the fritters in batches for 4–5 minutes until golden. Drain on kitchen paper. Sprinkle with sugar and serve immediately with cream and lemon wedges.

475 g (15 oz) can pineapple rings

425 g (14 oz) can apricot halves

flour, for dusting

oil, for deep-frying

caster sugar, to sprinkle

Batter:

125 g (4 oz) plain flour

pinch of mixed spice

pinch of salt

1 large egg, separated

150 ml (¼ pint) water

1 tablespoon oil

lemon wedges, to serve

| **Serves 4** |
| **Preparation time:** 15 minutes |
| **Cooking time:** 15 minutes |

poached figs

1 Place the wine, cassis, cinnamon sticks, citrus rind and water in a saucepan and bring to the boil.

2 Add the figs, cover the pan and simmer gently for 10 minutes until the figs are dark red and soft-ened. Do not over-cook or the figs will fall apart. Remove the figs with a slot-ted spoon and place in a serving dish. Bring the poaching liquid to a rolling boil and simmer until it is reduced by half and is thick and syrupy. Pour over the figs and leave to cool.

3 Meanwhile, combine all the sauce ingredients and set aside for the flavours to develop. Serve the figs at room temperature with a spoonful of sauce for each serving.

300 ml (½ pint) red wine

150 ml (¼ pint) cassis

2 cinnamon sticks

2 strips of lemon rind

2 strips of orange rind

300 ml (½ pint) water

12 large firm ripe figs, washed

Sauce:

150 g (5 oz) Greek yogurt

2 tablespoons clear Greek honey

1 teaspoon ground cinnamon

Serves 4
Preparation time: 10 minutes, plus cooling
Cooking time: 10 minutes

1 Place the sugar and 300 ml (½ pint) of the water in a pan over a low heat, stirring until the sugar has dissolved. Bring to the boil, add the blueberries, reduce the heat and simmer for 3–4 minutes. Using a slotted spoon, remove one-third of the berries to a bowl and reserve. Leave the remaining fruit to cool slightly in the syrup.

2 Purée the fruit and syrup in a liquidizer or process in a food mill. Strain into a clean pan. Taste and add more sugar if required. Bring to the boil, mix the arrowroot with the remaining water until well blended and whisk into the fruit purée; keep whisking until thickened.

3 Remove from the heat, stir in the reserved berries and leave to cool, stirring occasionally to prevent a skin from forming. Spoon into small bowls or glasses and chill thoroughly. Serve with the soured cream, if liked.

75 g (3 oz) caster sugar

600 ml (1 pint) water

500 g (1 lb) fresh blueberries

1½ tablespoons arrowroot

soured cream, to serve (optional)

Serves 4

Preparation time: 5 minutes, plus chilling

Cooking time: 10 minutes

blueberry kissel

cranachan
with fruit kissel

1 Pick over, wash and prepare the fruits if fresh. Frozen fruits need not be thawed. Place in a bowl.

2 Dissolve the sugar in the orange juice over a low heat. Mix the cornflour to a smooth paste with the water and add to the pan. Bring to the boil, stirring, until the sauce clears and thickens. Pour over the fruit and stir gently. Cover and chill in the refrigerator for at least 3 hours.

3 To make the cranachan, whip the two creams together until they form soft peaks. Add the vanilla, then fold in the sugar and all but 2 teaspoons of the toasted oatmeal. Spoon the cranachan into a serving dish and sprinkle with the reserved toasted oatmeal. Serve with the chilled kissel.

■ The kissel can be prepared up to 24 hours in advance and stored in the refrigerator.

Kissel:

500 g (1 lb) fresh or frozen soft fruits (choose 3–4 from raspberries, redcurrants, loganberries, strawberries, blackcurrants and blackberries)

50 g (2 oz) soft light brown sugar

150 ml (¼ pint) unsweetened orange juice

2 teaspoons cornflour

2 tablespoons water

Cranachan:

150 ml (¼ pint) double or whipping cream

150 ml (¼ pint) single cream

few drops of vanilla extract

1 tablespoon soft light brown sugar

40 g (1½ oz) coarse oatmeal, toasted

Serves 4

Preparation time: 20 minutes, plus chilling

Cooking time: 5 minutes

lemon syllabub

1 Place the lemon rind and juice in a bowl with the wine and half the sugar. Leave to soak for 1 hour.

2 Whip the cream until it stands in peaks, then gradually add the wine mixture and continue whipping until it holds its shape.

3 Whisk the egg white until stiff then whisk in the remaining sugar. Carefully fold into the cream mixture. Spoon into individual glasses and serve immediately with langue de chat biscuits.

grated rind and juice of 1 lemon

125 ml (4 fl oz) white wine

75 g (3 oz) caster sugar

300 ml (½ pint) double cream

1 egg white

langue de chat biscuits, to serve

Serves 4

Preparation time: 10 minutes, plus soaking

champagne syllabub
& strawberries

1 Mix together the champagne, sugar, and lemon rind and juice in a large bowl. Add the cream and whisk the mixture until it holds soft peaks. Spoon into glasses, then chill in the refrigerator for 1–2 hours before serving.

2 Serve the syllabub with a mixture of cultivated and wild strawberries, if possible.

150 ml (¼ pint) champagne or sparkling dry white wine

2 tablespoons caster sugar

finely grated rind and juice of ½ lemon

300 ml (½ pint) double cream

ripe strawberries, to serve

Serves 4

Preparation time: 5–10 minutes, plus chilling

pots au chocolat

1 Melt the chocolate by breaking it into pieces and placing it in a small bowl set over a pan of simmering water (make sure the water does not touch the bowl).

2 Add the orange rind, egg yolks and single cream to the bowl of melted chocolate and mix well. Stir in the Cointreau or orange juice. Whisk the egg whites until stiff and fold into the chocolate mixture.

3 Spoon into 4–6 small dishes and refrigerate until set. To serve, decorate with whipped cream and grated chocolate.

125 g (4 oz) plain chocolate

finely grated rind of ½ orange

3 eggs, separated

65 ml (2½ fl oz) single cream

1 tablespoon Cointreau or orange juice

To Decorate:

65 ml (2½ fl oz) whipping cream, whipped

grated chocolate

Serves 4–6

Preparation time: 10 minutes

Cooking time: about 5 minutes

■ If freezing, cover with foil when set and seal in a freezer bag. These will freeze for up to 6 weeks. Defrost in the refrigerator for 3-4 hours. Decorate as above and serve.

cinnamon & apple pudding

1 Melt the butter in a frying pan, add the breadcrumbs, cinnamon and demerara sugar and stir over a medium heat until crisp and toffee-like. Set aside to cool.

2 Poach the apples in the measured water with 1 tablespoon of the caster sugar. When soft, purée in a blender or food processor, or rub through a sieve. Set aside to cool.

3 Whip the cream with the remaining sugar until thick, then stir in the yogurt. In individual dishes or one large glass bowl, layer the apple, breadcrumbs and cream, ending with a layer of breadcrumbs. Chill, then serve decorated with whipped cream and chocolate.

75 g (3 oz) butter

200 g (7 oz) fresh breadcrumbs

2–3 teaspoons ground cinnamon

125 g (4 oz) demerara sugar

4 cooking apples, peeled, cored and quartered

125 ml (4 fl oz) water

3 tablespoons caster sugar

250 ml (8 fl oz) double cream

150 g (5 oz) natural yogurt

To Serve:

whipped cream

chocolate curls

Serves 4

Preparation time: 10 minutes, plus chilling

Cooking time: 10 minutes

strawberry crumble flan

1 Crumb the ginger biscuits in a food processor. Alternatively, place the biscuits between 2 large sheets of greaseproof paper and crush them with a heavy rolling pin. Melt the butter in a small saucepan, add the biscuit crumbs and mix well.

2 Press the crumb mixture over the base and sides of a loose-bottomed 20 cm (8 inch) flan tin. Chill the crumb case until set.

3 To make the filling, beat the cream cheese, caster sugar, grated lemon rind and cream in a bowl. Carefully transfer the chilled crumb case from the flan tin to a serving plate. Fill the case with the cream cheese mixture, smoothing the top. Arrange the strawberries on top. Dust with icing sugar and serve cold.

Crumb Case:

175 g (6 oz) ginger biscuits

75 g (3 oz) butter

Filling:

250 g (8 oz) cream cheese, softened

75 g (3 oz) caster sugar

1 teaspoon grated lemon rind

4 tablespoons single cream

375 g (12 oz) small strawberries, hulled, halved if large

icing sugar, for dusting

Serves 4–6

Preparation time: 20 minutes, plus chilling

Cooking time: 5 minutes

white chocolate soufflés

1 Use the melted butter to grease the sides of 6 individual 150 ml (¼ pint) ovenproof soufflé dishes. Place the dishes on a baking sheet.

2 Put the white chocolate in a heatproof bowl together with the double cream and the milk and then heat over a pan of simmering water until the chocolate has melted completely. Stir the mixture lightly to blend together.

3 Stir the sugar, egg yolks and vanilla extract into the chocolate and cream mixture. Whisk the egg whites in a large bowl until stiff and with soft but formed peaks. Using a large metal spoon, fold a quarter of the egg whites into the chocolate sauce, then fold in the remainder.

4 Spoon the mixture into the dishes, filling them almost to the rims, and place in a preheated oven, 200°C (400°F), Gas Mark 6, for 15–20 minutes until well risen and golden. Dust with cocoa powder or icing sugar and serve immediately.

5 g (¼ oz) unsalted butter, melted

250 g (8 oz) white chocolate, broken into pieces

50 ml (2 fl oz) double cream

25 ml (1 fl oz) milk

40 g (1½ oz) caster sugar

6 eggs, separated

1 teaspoon vanilla extract

cocoa powder or icing sugar, for dusting

Serves 6

Preparation time: 20 minutes

Cooking time: 20 minutes

chocolate rum truffles

1 Melt the chocolate in a bowl over a saucepan of simmering water. Remove from the heat and leave to cool.

2 Beat the butter and icing sugar together until light and fluffy. Add the cooled, melted chocolate and rum and stir until thoroughly combined. Cover and refrigerate the mixture until firm.

3 Remove the chocolate mixture from the refrigerator and shape the mixture into 2.5 cm (1 inch) balls. Roll each ball in the cocoa powder and place on a wax paper-lined baking sheet. Refrigerate the truffles until firm. Remove the truffles from the refrigerator and allow to stand at room temperature for 30 minutes before serving.

75 g (3 oz) plain chocolate, broken into pieces

25 g (1 oz) unsalted butter

125 g (4 oz) icing sugar, sifted

2 tablespoons dark rum

cocoa powder, for coating

Makes about 16

Preparation time: 30 minutes, plus cooling and chilling

Cooking time: 10 minutes

■ When melting chocolate over hot water, do not let the water reach boiling point, if too hot the chocolate may seize.

1 Line a baking sheet with non-stick baking parchment or greased greaseproof paper. Stir the ground almonds, caster sugar and almond essence into the egg whites. Place the mixture in a piping bag with a large star nozzle and pipe the mixture into circles. Put a piece of glacé cherry, or flaked almonds if preferred, on to each of the petits fours.

2 Place in a preheated oven, 150°C (300°F), Gas Mark 2, for 20–25 minutes. Cool on a wire rack.

125 g (4 oz) ground almonds

125 g (4 oz) caster sugar

few drops of almond essence

2 egg whites, whisked until stiff

glacé cherries or flaked almonds, to decorate

Makes about 24

Preparation time: 15 minutes

Cooking time: 20–25 minutes

almond petits fours

index